What to Say

TO A

Porcupine

What to Say
TO A
Porcupine

20 HUMOROUS TALES
THAT GET TO THE HEART OF
GREAT CUSTOMER SERVICE

Richard S. Gallagher

American Management Association

New York • Atlanta • Brussels • Chicago • Mexico City • San Francisco
Shanghai • Tokyo • Toronto • Washington, D.C.

Special discounts on bulk quantities of AMACOM books are
available to corporations, professional associations, and other
organizations. For details, contact Special Sales Department,
AMACOM, a division of American Management Association,
1601 Broadway, New York, NY 10019.
Tel.: 212-903-8316.   Fax: 212-903-8083.
Website: www.amacombooks.org

This publication is designed to provide accurate and authoritative
information in regard to the subject matter covered. It is sold with the
understanding that the publisher is not engaged in rendering legal,
accounting, or other professional service. If legal advice or other expert
assistance is required, the services of a competent professional person
should be sought.

Library of Congress Cataloging-in-Publication Data

Gallagher, Richard S.
    What to say to a porcupine : 20 humorous tales that get to the heart /
of Great Customer Service Richard S. Gallagher.
        p.   cm.
    Includes index.
    ISBN-13: 978-0-8144-1055-4
    ISBN-10: 0-8144-1055-3
        1. Customer services—Humor.   2. Customer services—Management—Humor.
    3. Customer relations—Humor.   I. Title.

    HF5415.5.G353   2008
    658.8'12—dc22

                                                                    2008008103

Printing number

10   9   8   7   6   5   4   3   2   1

To Colleen, my most blessed customer relationship

Contents

Section II
On the Front Lines

Section III
R-E-S-P-E-C-T

Contents

Acknowledgments

To my nieces and nephews Katie, Annie, Richard, and Henry—your giggles were the best editorial feedback I could ever ask for. Thank you for teaching me that you are never too young—or too old—to be a storyteller.

To everyone in my family—thank you as always for your love and support.

To my literary agent Diana Finch, Executive Editor Ellen Kadin, and the entire team at AMACOM—it is an honor and a pleasure to work with all of you once again.

To my wife Colleen—you were the one who believed in this project from the get-go and told me that I absolutely had to write this book. The fact that I am madly in love with you doesn't hurt, either.

Finally, to all of my readers, old and new—may your own service to others be a source of joy and laughter every day.

Introduction

The vast majority of us spend much of our lives serving other people. More than half of us work directly with the public, while nearly everyone has so-called internal customer relationships with others in the workplace. It is a big part, perhaps the biggest part, of our working lives. But, sadly, there is often a singular lack of good humor in the way we discuss the art of customer service.

More often, this topic is a fertile breeding ground for lectures that are reminiscent of what many parents tell their children: Be nice to people. Say please and thank you. Do unto others as you would do unto yourself—etcetera. These lectures are usually received with the same (lack of) enthusiasm as the parental version, with the net result that service quality doesn't change and people don't learn skills that help them become successful in their lives and careers.

That's where this book comes in. My goal is to have a little fun with the things that happen between you and your customers—and, in the process, share some of the real secrets of serving other people. In it, you will learn how to make a great first impression, what to do when things go wrong, and positive ways to coach your service team—and, of course, what to say to a porcupine!

..... Introduction

In the process, I follow a storytelling tradition that dates back thousands of years. Following the format of the classic Aesop's Fables, these vignettes use animals and humans to tell an entertaining story, and then share a moral that you can use in your life. Moreover, the storylines of many of these fables spring from research into how these very animals or groups of people actually behave in real life—making their lessons not only humorous, but accurate as well.

When I was developing my previous book, *Great Customer Connections,* which looks at the psychology of how we interact with customers, I was struck by the depth of skills that are needed to handle most customer situations. The best practitioners treat it as a noble craft—and when people are taught this craft, there is no limit to how far they can go.

The twenty tales in this book will teach you the secrets of this craft, in a way that no serious textbook ever could. I hope that they succeed in making you laugh. But more important, I hope they succeed in making you succeed. Enjoy!

Richard S. Gallagher

Section I
The Basics

· 1 ·

Send in the Clowns

Some clowns were sitting around a conference table, with serious looks on their grease-painted faces, as they met with a consultant at their local small business development center.

Bubbles, a six-foot-tall clown with a huge mop of purple hair, spoke up first. "Back when we were with the circus, we used to chase one another around the big top," he said. "But nowadays, we haven't been so good at chasing business."

"Hmm. How bad are your business problems?" said the consultant.

"Let's just say that if we don't figure out something soon, wearing these tramp suits isn't going to be an act anymore," replied Bubbles.

"So why did you folks start this business, anyway?"

"The circus owners decided that we didn't fit their strategic plan anymore," sighed Bonzo, one of the other clowns. "As they put it, 'Elephants don't need fringe benefits.' Anyway, we decided to start our own clown-for-hire business. You know, the usual stuff—corporate work, hospitals, perhaps a few private parties here and there."

"I see," the consultant intoned. "Are you having trouble getting leads?"

"I'll say! When we go to marketing events, people always seem to hightail it away from us faster than you can say *wowie kazowie*."

"Well, let's sit down and examine this situation," replied the consultant. As he took his seat, the unmistakable sound of a whoopee cushion filled the room—which immediately got the consultant thinking. Looking intently at each of the clowns, he said, "Tell me more about these marketing events. What happens when a potential customer comes over to talk with you folks?"

"Well, we usually spray them with seltzer," Bonzo replied. "But it just doesn't seem to work."

"Honking our big red horns in their ears doesn't do the trick, either," Bubbles noted dourly. "We thought it was funny until we tried it with a police group, and we all got charged with disorderly conduct."

Then the consultant said, "I think I see the problem. It's your first impressions on customers. You are acting like a bunch of clowns!"

The clowns looked at one another with mock surprise as Buster replied, "Well, duh-uh."

The consultant continued unfazed. "You see, when someone is looking to hire a clown, it's all about them, not you. They want a good time. They want to make their kids happy, or impress their clients. They've got needs to fill. And you're all too busy clowning around to notice."

"So we can't just be ourselves?" Bubbles asked, sheepishly.

"To quote one of my favorite childhood TV shows, that's a Bozo no-no," replied the consultant. "You need to focus on making a good first impression on your customers—right out of the starting gate. If you don't, you may never get a second chance."

For the rest of the session, the consultant held a serious discussion—at least, as serious as one can have in a room full of clowns—on strategies to create a good initial impression. The recommendations ranged from how to introduce themselves to the finer points of negotiating a sales contract. As things wrapped up for the afternoon, the consultant offered them one final piece of advice: "Oh, by the way—those big red clown shoes and the rubber noses? Gotta go. Save the getup for after you sign the contract."

"But it worked for Ronald McDonald!" wailed Bubbles.

"Look . . . make a DVD of yourselves in action, and then get a suit," the consultant said sharply. "And this"—he continued, holding up the deflated whoopee cushion—"isn't even funny."

• • •

Six months later, the same clowns—now looking very distinguished in their dark suits and ties—gathered for a much happier follow-up meeting with the same consultant.

"So, how's it going, Bubbles?" he asked, turning to greet their leader.

"You can call me Fred now," he replied with a smile. "Things couldn't be going better. Nowadays, our corporate motto is, 'We are serious about entertaining you,' and we pride ourselves on taking a professional, strategic approach to planning customer events."

"Excellent!" the consultant said. "Has it improved your business?"

"Beyond our wildest dreams," Fred replied, as the others nodded in unison. "We've gone from being a bunch of clowns to becoming corporate and residential entertainment specialists. And you are now looking at the management team of a very large and growing enterprise."

The consultant, visibly impressed, clapped Fred on the back. "That is fantastic! I'm impressed that you were able to turn your business around so well. Tell me, do you folks ever miss acting like clowns?"

"Well, just this once," Fred smiled. "We recently bought out the circus where we used to work, and we're just about to meet with our old CEO to discuss the new business strategy." As the others around the table pulled out their horns and seltzer bottles, he continued, "We're going to have a lot of fun with that meeting. But you were absolutely right—success really is a matter of knowing when to be yourselves."

Moral: *Make a Good First Impression*

You have thirty seconds to make an impression on someone—and that initial impression will govern a customer's reactions from then on. That's why smart companies from all walks of life work hard to make the most of those first thirty seconds. For example:

- When you hire a moving company, your first visit usually isn't from someone in grubby work clothes—more likely it's a pleasant person wearing a suit, stopping by to discuss your needs for the move.

- When you visit the dentist, she probably doesn't start the visit by talking about your teeth at all—more likely, she will ask questions or make small talk designed to put you at ease.

- Even online customer support centers are often trained to respond to your problems by typing messages that welcome you warmly and offer to be helpful.

Realize that it's all about the customer—and when businesses put themselves in that customer's mind-set, right from the start, they get that much more of a chance to be the best at what they do.

Discussion Questions

* What kind of image do you want to convey to your customers?

* What is the difference between focusing on your expertise versus your customers' needs?

* What kinds of things can you do—and say—with customers to make it "all about them"?

· 2 ·

Running with the Pack

Most people are familiar with the expression "laughing like a hyena." But at Hyena's Desert Grille—an upscale casual-dining establishment run by several hyenas from a neighborhood pack—things were no laughing matter. Business had been falling off for several months, and they were now running perilously close to their break-even point. And worse, no one really seemed to know why.

It wasn't always this way. Hyena's used to be known as *the* place for carnivores to have a good time over a spit of roast prey and pitchers of draft beer. In its heyday, there were lines of creatures spilling out onto the sidewalk every weekend. But over the past year, the crowds had gotten smaller. There was no new competition and no other obvious reason for the decline. As Jocko, the general manager, put it, "Hey, we are what we are." But even Jocko knew that something had to be done, and soon.

So, they brought in a consultant—a motivational speaker on customer service. She was perky, bubbly, and armed with boxes of books and tapes. Before long, she gathered the whole restaurant staff together to lecture them about the benefits of having a great attitude.

"The first rule is to always smile, smile, smile!" she exclaimed.

"But we already smile," sighed Ernie, the assistant manager. "Remember, we're all hyenas."

Undaunted, she continued, extolling the virtues of customer passion, creating magical moments, and being a winner. And then she left.

Unfortunately, nothing changed in the days and weeks that followed—so they brought in another consultant. This one, a funny-looking man with a white shirt and thick glasses, had all sorts of measurements, stopwatches, and some strange tool called "customer relationship management." By the time this consultant left, their wallets were several thousand dollars lighter, and they were now the proud owners of a state-of-the-art computer system that could tell them in micrometric detail how productive each server was, how many pounds of gazelle were on order, and what customers ordered every night.

Still, none of it helped Hyena's get more customers in the door. So they decided to bring in one more consultant. He didn't give them a motivational speech. Nor did he measure anything. In fact, he just sat in a corner booth, ordered the Grilled Antelope Caesar Salad, and took notes—for a *long* time. And then he did something that seemed even stranger: He began wandering from table to table, chatting amiably with the customers—a pit bull and his two sons, a young wolf dining alone, a family of cougars, and even a group of aging female brown bears who wore red hats and were laughing loudly over their piña coladas.

Hours later, as the restaurant was closing up for the evening, the consultant gathered Jocko and his fellow managers around a table in the back. "So, tell me, what were you doing out there on the floor today?" began Jocko.

"I was watching what happened between you and your patrons in the course of a normal work day," the consultant replied. "Then I went around and talked with your customers—and more important— I *listened* to them. As a result, I think I have a pretty good picture of what's going on these days with your restaurant."

"Interesting. Tell me more," said Jocko.

"First of all, while I was eating lunch, I observed your team in action. You all basically seem like nice guys and gals overall. But one thing really stuck out. Whenever someone complained about the food, or wanted a better table, or had any other kind of problem, you all seemed a little . . . shall we say . . . aggressive."

"Of course we're aggressive—don't you understand? We're predators," said Jocko, with some visible exasperation.

"And pack animals" chimed in Ernie. "Surely our customers must understand the whole instinct thing, don't they?"

"Let me put it this way," the consultant said. "Are customers complaining about the wait to get in these days?"

"They used to," said Ernie with a sigh.

"Then I think you've just answered your own question. And later, when I was chatting with one of the regulars, she talked about the time that a family of woodchucks came in looking for a place to have lunch."

"Oh, yes . . ." Jocko said, rolling his eyes.

"You ate them—in front of the customers," said the consultant.

"Look, you're a human, right? What would you do if a juicy young chicken landed in your yard?"

"I guess the whole point is that you shouldn't be putting yourselves first. Even among humans, doing things like eating, drinking, or gossiping in front of customers just doesn't look classy. And besides," the consultant sighed, "restaurants normally *order* food these days."

"Bottom line," he continued, "I see something going on that I see in a lot of businesses that were once successful. You start focusing on yourselves and not your customers. You have lots of rules nowadays. You say absolutely no substitutions, and you require the whole party to be here before anyone can be seated. Even though your patrons are mostly predators, you don't allow hunting on the premises. And above all, when customers have problems, you unknowingly act like they should feel privileged to eat here."

"So, we started reacting to our success, as opposed to the people who made us successful," said Jocko thoughtfully.

"Exactly correct," smiled the consultant. "Fortunately, it's easily fixed, in my experience. Oh, and one more thing . . ."

"Yes?"

"Your wait staff *laughs* at people when they take their orders."

"But we always laugh. We're all hyenas," replied Ernie.

"Don't worry; it's nothing that a little training won't fix."

• • •

A few weeks later, after some more work with the consultant and a series of focus groups in the predator community, Hyena's managers had a pretty good handle on why customers were falling away faster than prey on the run. More important, they used what they learned to improve their service. Old rules were revised, a new staff training program was implemented, and even their trademark cackling laughs got replaced by a friendly chuckle. They started reaching out to the community, with events like football night with free appetizers and entrails, and a monthly women's "Running with the Wolves" luncheon. Above all, Hyena's was once again a place where carnivores could count on great food and a good time—and soon enough, the crowds started coming back.

One Saturday night, a few months later, Jocko surveyed his crowded restaurant and overheard a group of young jackals say, "Man,

Hyena's is definitely the place to be on a Saturday night." He couldn't resist walking over and asking them what they liked about his restaurant, and one of them replied, "This place is cool. You guys always make our pack feel at home." Just then, he made eye contact with another family of woodchucks making their way across the parking lot. He smiled, waved at them, and returned to the kitchen with that knowing look that comes from experience.

Moral: *Listen to Your Customers*

Does service quality really matter when it comes to keeping customers, versus "real" things like your restaurant's food and menu selection or the price of your merchandise? Statistically, yes. Studies have shown that high customer satisfaction levels yield results ranging from greater profitability and lower marketing expenses to higher stock prices.

Moving from fables to the real world, you can often see a direct link between service quality and crowd size at many of the places where you eat. For example, different restaurants in the same chain often have wildly different levels of success depending on how customers are treated. More important, the fortunes of the same restaurant can change dramatically with even subtle changes in how customers perceive the level of service, *even when the food is exactly the same.* When employees are unmotivated and customers don't come first, crowds usually get smaller and smaller until these restaurants eventually go out of business. And much like these fictional hyenas, the restaurant owners probably never even understand why.

You can change this dynamic by making a habit of asking customers what they think, and then using this feedback to improve your operations. No matter what profession you are in, input from your customers holds the keys to your success. Listen to what they tell you—and more important, react to it—and you will be at the top of your game in any business.

Discussion Questions

✳ How much input does your organization seek from your customers?

✳ How do you use feedback from customers, and are your people on the front line fully aware of what customers are saying?

✳ Do customer comments—including criticism—lead to real changes in your policies and procedures?

· 3 ·

My Big Fat Greek Chorus

"This place would be great if it wasn't for all these stupid customers," Sandy thought as she cleaned up another mess at one of the tables of her family's snack bar. It seemed like all day she was constantly fighting a losing battle to keep people in line. "Keep your kids from running around, please." "For the fourth time, we can't do special orders." "We're closing in ten minutes." As she ran over to keep another kid from tipping over the gumball machine, she thought to herself that this wasn't much different from when she used to work in the school system as a lunch monitor.

Today, in particular, she couldn't wait for her shift to end, because tonight was her night out with Elsie. Every month, the two of them planned something new and different. For Sandy, these nights out were a needed break from the grind of the snack bar. Tonight, they were going to see a play at the local performing arts center—a well-reviewed modern interpretation of a Greek tragedy.

A few hours later, the two of them were finally settled in their seats at the theater. As the curtain rose, Sandy whispered softly to Elsie, "Who are all those people in togas, gathered at the side of the stage?"

"They call them a Greek chorus," replied Elsie. "I was reading in the program that they are sort of like the voice of the audience. They follow the actors around and comment on what they are doing." And sure enough, whatever the main characters were doing, the Greek chorus added their two cents in song, in a way that was hilarious to the audience. "This is kind of like having your mother constantly follow you around," chuckled Elsie, as Sandy nodded in agreement.

Later that night, after she fell asleep, Sandy had a very strange dream: She was shopping, and the Greek chorus from the play was constantly following her around the store, singing in unison about everything she was doing. "Touchest that not." "Putteth that back." "Hurry up, our break hath started." As they kept watching her, fingers pointing in unison at her, the scene was abruptly cut off by the high-pitched buzz of Sandy's alarm clock.

Later that afternoon, back at the snack bar, it was another busy day. As one customer came to the register to pay his check, Sandy looked up to spy his little boy running down one of the aisles with his arms flailing. Flashing a look of annoyed resignation at the customer, she instinctively headed over toward the kid, sighing to herself, "Can't people keep an eye on these little monsters?"

Suddenly, she glanced over the racks of potato chips, and there they were—the faces of the Greek chorus, staring intently at her, as plain as day. As she looked back at them, they said nothing, but kept their gaze fixed silently on her. Turning as white as a sheet, she walked around the aisle, stood in front of them, and started to stammer. "Are . . . are you . . . ?"

Before she could finish, one of them replied, "Hi! We're on our way to do a theater performance and we're really hungry. Could you pack up some hot dogs and soda to go for us?" The other actors, dressed in their street clothes, smiled and nodded in unison.

Sandy, still shaking, placed their orders and then returned to the cash register, where the first customer said, "Were you about to tell me something?" "Yes," she replied thoughtfully. "What a beautiful little son you have! I'm really glad you both came in today. Have a nice day!"

The acting troupe, sandwiches and sodas in hand, filed silently out. As the glass door of the snack bar swung shut behind them, the leader of the group turned around, smiled at the others, winked, and quietly said, "Mission accomplished!"

Moral: *Don't Hassle Your Customers*

People aren't perfect because they are, well, people. This means that if you work with the public, it is a given that children will scream, people will let their bad moods show, and picky customers will make demands on you.

This reality presents a subtle but important challenge for anyone who works in customer service. On the one hand, it is perfectly okay to set legitimate boundaries, such as asking children not to damage merchandise or grown-ups to stop screaming at you. On the other hand, if life's normal imperfections constantly get under your skin, you may find yourself unwittingly deep-sighing your way through your entire workday—and in time, develop a mindset that leads to poor service.

The solution to this problem is simple, but takes practice: Start expecting customers to behave like people, and learn to keep your sense of humor about those "moments" that seem to happen all too frequently. In time, you'll find that you will not just give people a good experience, but you will have a much better time on the job yourself. So be kind to others—even during those moments when you are tempted to bite your lip—and watch your service soar.

Discussion Questions

* How often do you and your team "vent" about customer situations?

* How can you keep frustrations about customers from boiling over into too many rules and too much negativity?

* What can you do to show your appreciation to the vast majority of people who purchase your products and services?

· 4 ·

Squawk!

The usual gang of parrots were having a night out at a local tropical bar, like they did every Thursday night, and after a couple of hours the liquor and the conversation were flowing freely.

Of course, the conversation part always posed a bit of a challenge. Parrots are very smart birds, but when it comes to communicating with one another in English, they can only repeat phrases that they have learned from their human owners. Nonetheless, they usually know enough phrases to cobble together a reasonable conversation. Tonight, the topic was how they could learn more tricks to impress their owners and get more bird treats.

Peppy, who was owned by a motivational speaker, was characteristically positive about it. "It's a great day. Let's go for it. We can all reach for the stars!"

Stocky, whose owner was a manager for a major chain store, chimed in, "We can make a plan. We can track our progress. We're always improving our operations."

Buzzy, a local artist's pet, lifted his beak from a clawful of bar peanuts and spoke up, too. "Cool man. That's really wild."

Finally Rudy, who was owned by a small shopkeeper, weighed in on the plan. "You can't do that. It's not our policy. No refunds. Awwwk!"

The other parrots, accustomed to this kind of behavior from Rudy, tried their best to placate him. "Have another margarita," cooed Buzzy. "Sorry, no food or drink allowed!" retorted Rudy.

"Let's get back to work," implored Stocky. "How can you expect me to get any work done these days? You can't find any good help anymore," shot back Rudy.

By this time, even the ever-upbeat Peppy was feeling a little frustrated. Cocking his right eye toward Rudy, he said firmly, "It's time to start taking some personal responsibility for success!" Staring straight back at Peppy and not missing a beat, Rudy exclaimed, "This problem is your fault. Squawwwk!"

After a few more minutes of this back-and-forth with Rudy, the other three birds finally huddled together while he was taking a break in the birds' room, and they came up with a plan. Or, to be more accurate, two plans. First, they sketched out some new tricks to rehearse before their next night at the bar. The second plan dealt directly with Rudy right then and there—his beak now stuffed with napkins by the other birds, he could only manage a muffled, "Don't touch the merchandise!" as the others hashed out the details for their next get-together.

Soon the evening drew to a close and the other birds finally unstuffed Rudy, still flapping and sputtering. As they headed for the door, Buzzy turned sympathetically toward Rudy and said, "Everyone feels like squawking sometimes." Rudy brightened once again and nodded enthusiastically.

Moral: *Avoid Negative Expectation*

Let's see a show of hands—how many of you readers are rude people? Just as I expected, very few of you raised your hands. Yet rude service certainly does exist—and a lot more frequently than we care to admit.

One of the reasons that we run into so many rude people in service is a phenomenon called "negative expectation." In layman's terms, it means that we assume the worst in other people, and then end up communicating in a negative and self-protective way that irritates everyone we deal with—which, in turn, does nothing but strengthen these negative stereotypes.

Our feathered friend (aptly and intentionally named "Rude-y") responds to polite overtures from others with presumptive statements that, in all likelihood, were forged from his own previous bad experiences: "That's not our policy." "No food or drink allowed." "You can't find good help anymore." Before you know it, you have a mind-set that leads you to squawk at everything—and lose customers and profits.

Try an experiment tomorrow. Check what you say to people in the course of a workday, and if too much of it sounds like Rudy, see what a difference it makes when you lighten up and give people the benefit of the doubt. When you learn to treat customers like the great people most of them are, the rewards will come back to you many times over.

Discussion Questions

* Can you think of any situations where people in your organization assume the worst about customers, and show it?

* Are your policies customer-friendly, or do they show mistrust and negativity toward them?

* How can you change the mechanics of how you communicate with customers and what you say to them, to make them feel cherished and appreciated?

· **5** ·

The Snipe Hunt

nother boring Saturday morning, thought Timmy, scrunched defiantly in the back seat of his family's minivan as they headed for their weekly trip to the mall. As Dad drove, Mom chattered nonstop about people in the neighborhood. "That Loretta . . . ," she said. "What a snipe she is!"

Timmy's ears perked up at the sound of a new word. "Mom! Dad! What's a snipe?"

His father smiled and winked knowingly at his wife, and then looked at his son in the rearview mirror. "Ah, yes, the snipe! It's a very mysterious creature that is famous around these parts. It's big, and spotted, and runs around the forest."

Timmy's eyes grew wide as his dad continued. "In fact, when I was your age, my friends and I used to go on snipe hunts all the time! You'd wait in the woods with a big paper bag, and your friends would chase 'em with their flashlights. If you got lucky, one of them would run right into your bag!"

"D'ya ever catch one?" Timmy said excitedly.

"Oh, yes," his mother chimed in with a smile. "Harvey was one of the best snipe hunters in the whole county."

"An' how d'ya know it was a snipe, Dad?" he said.

"Because they're so ornery," Dad replied. "The most mean-spirited critter you've ever met. If it's big, and spotted, and ornery, you've definitely got a snipe on your hands. But if you catch one, you're the hero of the whole neighborhood."

"Wow," said Timmy. "I wanna catch snipes just like you, Dad!"

Soon they were all at the mall, where Timmy stood impatiently with his father in the massive Jingle and Company department store while his mother tried on dresses. Soon he wandered off as his father was reading the paper, and when his mother came out, she turned to her husband and said, "Where's Timmy?"

Before he could answer, a loud commotion erupted a couple of aisles away. They rushed over to find an older sales clerk, in a bright-pink spotted dress, shrieking and struggling with a shopping bag that had been put over her head. As the store manager hurried to the scene, Timmy gleefully continued to hold the bag down and proudly exclaimed, "Mom, Dad, look—I caught a snipe! A *big* one!"

"A snipe?" asked the store manager, a quizzical look on his face.

"Yeah. My dad tol' me that snipes were big, an' spotted, an' ornery," replied Timmy, as the clerk finally wrestled the bag off of her head. Then he puckered up his face and faithfully mimicked what he heard from the sales clerk. "I can't help you now, I'm going on break. . . . If you want to know what's on sale, read the signs. . . . No, we don't have any other colors in stock." Finally, lowering his voice to a stage whisper, he continued: "Can't these stupid customers even find a shirt on the rack themselves?"

Everyone around him now broke out laughing—except the sales clerk, whose face turned pinker than her dress. The store manager turned to her and said firmly, "Doris . . ." She quickly replied, "All right, George, I'm sorry. I was having a really bad day, and I shouldn't have taken it out on our customers. I'll be more polite to everyone from now on." With a sidelong glance at Timmy, she added, "It sure beats having little kids put bags over your head."

The store manager then turned to Timmy and his parents. "You know, son, we're always trying to keep snipes out of our store, too. Of course," he said, nodding toward Doris, "we usually do it a little less publicly. But I have to give you credit for what you've taught us today. Would you folks like to talk about this over some ice cream sundaes in the store restaurant? They're on the house."

"Yes! An' be sure to talk to my dad, because he's an even better snipe hunter than I am," exclaimed Timmy, as everyone laughed. "Then it's a deal," the manager replied. "Let's go!"

Moral: *Don't Be a Snipe*

There is one problem with customer service. Customers generally don't come up to us to tell us what a great day they are having and what nice people we are. Customer service involves helping people with problems—and problems are no fun.

Because of this, it can become all too easy to follow human nature and respond negatively to people's problems. In time, these kinds of responses can become ingrained in us. But there are always diplomatic ways to say things in undiplomatic situations. Let's take what the clerk in our story said:

"I can't help you now, I'm going on break."

"If you want to know what's on sale, read the signs."

"No, we don't have any other colors in stock."

Now, let's see how we could reword things while saying exactly the same thing:

"Absolutely, I can get someone to help you."

"We've put up some signs to make it easy to find our best bargains today."

"I wish we had more colors in stock, but here are some really nice ones on the floor."

Can you always agree with people, or give them exactly what they want? No. But with practice, it's easy to learn how to never, ever be a snipe.

Discussion Questions

* Is anyone in your organization a "snipe" who is curt and snippy with customers?

* Do managers in your organization simply criticize people who act like "snipes," or do they take the time to coach and mentor them?

* How well do you train people on what to say—and not say—to customers?

Section II
On the Front Lines

· **6** ·

What to Say to a Porcupine

veryone knows that porcupines are fairly prickly. But if you aren't an animal, you probably didn't realize that they are also rude and demanding. That explains why, after a large colony of them settled into a quiet forest, things were never quite the same.

At first, local businesses went out of their way to welcome the porcupines. But soon, these large and extremely vocal rodents were making their presence felt all over town. The rowdy teenage porcupines would puff up their quills and scare other customers. Then there were the parents with no interest in reining in their young from gnawing the bark off of trees. There was even an elderly female porcupine who loudly demanded to be seen first every time she went to the forest clinic. In time, they were the talk of the forest.

Some of the other forest inhabitants tried in vain to argue with them—and soon, they discovered that challenging a porcupine usually resulted in hard feelings on both sides, if not a faceful of sharp quills. Others tried giving in to their ceaseless demands. But that didn't work, either. It simply wasn't practical; nor was it fair to their other customers.

Soon, porcupines were clearly on top of the agenda at the forest's monthly merchants meeting, held in the back room of one of the local stores. At first, some of the merchants debated new rules, such as limiting animals with quills from entering their stores. One buzzard, who ran a bar and grill in one of the rougher parts of the forest, even hinted darkly about "his boys" raising some mischief around the dead tree that these porcupines all lived under. Everyone agreed that something had to be done, and the sooner the better.

Then a wise owl, who had recently trained to become an animal psychologist, spoke up. "I've studied how to get along with difficult animals. The problem here is that we're all following our instinct— we're all fighting a species that is never, ever going to stop fighting back. There is another way to handle situations like this," the owl said, "but it means going against our natural instincts."

"Hey, if it wasn't for instinct, we wouldn't be animals!" piped up one of the squirrels in the back of the room. "I don't see why we have to change who we are just to accommodate these poor excuses for mammals."

As the owl started to respond, a burly middle-aged porcupine lumbered inside the store, oblivious to the "Closed for lunch" sign hanging on the door. Looking at the crowd assembled in the back room, he bellowed, "When am I going to get any service around here?" The owl whispered, "Let me handle this," and made her way to the front of the store to join the porcupine.

"About time someone showed up," said the porcupine gruffly.

"Hello, my friend," said the owl, "It's really frustrating when businesses close for lunch, isn't it? Tell me, what is your name?"

"Uh, I'm Elmer," he said, a little surprised.

"Pleased to meet you, Elmer. I'm Dr. Owl, from the merchant's association," she said, clasping his paw politely with her talon. "I'm glad you came to our store."

"I didn't know that you guys were closed for lunch," replied Elmer, taken somewhat off guard by her courtesy.

"Silly us—we should have made the sign on the door a lot bigger. I'm really sorry about that. This happens every month, when the merchants meet. Perhaps we should try to meet after business hours in the future. I'll certainly talk to the merchants about it for the future."

"So, when do you think someone could help me? I really need to get home to the kids," Elmer said, no longer sounding belligerent.

"We want you to get home as soon as possible, so, tell you what—how about I personally make sure that someone comes out of the meeting within the next fifteen minutes? In the meantime," said the owl, "why don't you make yourself at home on the couch over here, and help yourself to some coffee. And we've got some books and magazines here to read if you'd like."

"Well . . . okay. Um, thank you"

"No problem at all, my friend—have a great afternoon," said the owl with a smile, as she turned back toward the meeting.

"You too," nodded Elmer.

Closing the door behind her, Dr. Owl addressed the other forest merchants, who were now sitting in rapt attention after watching this encounter from afar. "Let me ask you all a question," she started. "Did I give in to the porcupine's demands to get helped immediately?"

"No," replied everyone.

"So why do you think that our friend is now sitting politely on the couch, waiting for the meeting to end?"

After an awkward pause, one of the rabbits spoke up: "Because you were nice to him."

Then the buzzard chimed in, "And you acted like his feelings mattered."

"Exactly correct!" replied Dr. Owl. "I spoke to his agenda. That's precisely what I mean about going against our instinct." Grabbing a marker, she strode over to a flipchart. "Let's break this down. Your store is closed. Someone walks in. What is the logical thing that most of us would say?"

"We're closed!" responded the squirrel.

"That's my point. The store being closed is *our* agenda, not the customer's. So that should not be the first thing that we say." Making notes on the board as she spoke, the owl continued. "In this case, the porcupine had a different agenda: First, he wasn't happy that no one was there to help him, and second, he wanted to get home as soon as possible. So, I addressed both of those things from the start. I promised to discuss the meeting times with you—which, by the way, we should discuss—and promised to get someone out there as soon as possible."

"So, you're saying that we should think a little more like a porcupine?" replied the buzzard.

"It does feel a little counterintuitive, especially when someone is rude and abrasive. But look at the results—you now have a calm and polite customer waiting outside, and I'm not wearing any quills!"

For the rest of the meeting, and in the days and weeks to come, Dr. Owl taught everyone how to speak to porcupines in all sorts of situations—from telling their kids to behave, to asking them to wait their turn—in ways that still focused on the porcupines' agendas and made them feel good. Soon everyone caught on and started to find ways to treat their spiny neighbors with deference and courtesy while still maintaining appropriate boundaries.

The results far exceeded everyone's expectations—and in time, the merchants learned that while porcupines were demanding, they were also loyal repeat customers with plenty to spend. Soon, the forest was even holding a Porcupine Appreciation Day sales event, with balloons for the kids to pop and their favorite quill pens on sale at a deep discount.

As Dr. Owl put it, "Nowadays, we've learned to handle prickly situations without getting ourselves stuck."

Moral: *Never Confront Someone Who Is Prickly*

Most of us aren't likely to match wits with a porcupine anytime soon. But if you work with the public, prickly characters are a universal fact of life. And ironically, human nature leads us to handle most of them exactly the wrong way—by challenging them.

This innate reaction stems from our natural survival instinct: We respond to threats by preparing ourselves to fight or flee. Unfortunately, while both of these instincts would probably be great reactions for a caveman faced with a hungry predator, they rarely serve us well with customers.

Instead, try using a little reverse psychology to speak to your customers' agendas, and watch what happens. The results are often nothing short of miraculous. For example:

It's human nature to say:	"Sorry, we don't give cash refunds."
It's better to say:	"I'm sorry you didn't like that. I have some great merchandise that we could exchange this item for."

—*or*—

It's human nature to say: "No, you can't go first—we have other people on line."

It's better to say: "I can tell you're in a rush. I'm going to finish serving everyone else on this line as quickly as I can."

By setting yourself up as an ally to a demanding customer, you are more likely to wrap things up quickly and easily—without giving in to unreasonable demands. So, next time you are faced with "porcupines," try seeing the world through their eyes and respond in kind. You may be amazed at their response!

Discussion Questions

* What kinds of "prickly" customers do you and your team deal with?

* What can you say to your difficult customers to empathize with them and get them on your side?

* Do people on your team know how to handle customer frustrations without taking them personally?

· 7 ·

Bear with Me

Some people think that bears hoard honey before they hibernate for the winter. In reality, they usually purchase it, much like humans do. And for as long as anyone can remember, a small shop run by Adam—a grizzly—provided for the needs of everyone in the local forest.

Before winter descended, it was pretty much the same ritual every year. Bears would line up outside Adam's store with whatever goodies they had hunted or scavenged. As they came to the head of the line, they would point to whatever honey they wanted, growl, and Adam would arch his furry eyebrows and growl back. A trade was quickly negotiated, and the honey was then heaved with a sturdy forepaw in the direction of the purchaser.

One by one, they dropped off their treasures—fat squirrels, fresh salmon, ripe berries and nuts—in return for a winter's supply of their favorite sweet treat. But then one gaunt, aging bear finally reached the head of the line with something else entirely—a book.

Adam was not amused. Books were occasionally interesting, but they weren't very tasty. He growled with annoyance as he pointed to a pile of fresh meat and another of succulent fruit. The elderly bear shook his head dejectedly and pointed at the book. He was clearly too old to hunt or forage anymore, and this book was all he had to offer. They kept staring at each other until finally, in frustration, Adam swiped the book with his paw and hurled the smallest jar of honey he had at the old bear, who caught it gingerly and shuffled out of the store.

After the shop had closed down for the night, Adam growled to himself as he picked up the book. Pushing his reading glasses farther back on his snout, he opened to the first chapter: "How to Greet Your Customers." Glancing quickly through the chapter, he nodded silently as he ran his right paw along the pages, before turning out the light and going to bed.

Still not entirely convinced, Adam decided to try an experiment the next morning. Instead of growling back, he said a hearty "Good morning!" to each bear who came into his shop. By the end of that week, he observed something interesting—the lines were noticeably longer.

The next week, he read Chapter 2: "How to Personalize Your Service." The next day at the shop, he started using everyone's name— and again, by the end of the week, the lines were longer still. Now quickly going through the other chapters, he began making other changes to his style: thanking people, learning what kinds of honey they liked best, and even getting to know the names of their cubs.

By the time he finished the book, the lines at his store had doubled in length! And something else interesting was happening as well: The other bears weren't growling anymore, and they were now bringing even more goodies in exchange for his honey.

One day a couple of weeks later, as winter drew near, the elderly bear who gave Adam the book was shuffling past his store on his way back from the senior center. As he passed by the doorway, he felt a firm paw clasp him on the back and drag him inside. Moments later, he emerged with a dazed look on his face, dragging a ten gallon case of honey, as Adam's voice trailed behind him. "Good to see you again, sir, and have a nice day!"

Moral: *Good Service Is All in the Mechanics*

There is a saying that you catch more flies with honey than vinegar. In this story, as in real life, you can get more of this honey in the first place by paying attention to what you say to people.

The mechanics of good customer relations go far beyond being polite and friendly to other people. There is an art and a science to how we interact with people, with roots dating back to the fundamentals of behavioral psychology. How we greet people, what we say to start and build customer relationships, and how we handle problems depend on using the right techniques every bit as much as they depend on your attitude.

There is no lack of good information out there on the mechanics of good service. Learn from it, change the fundamentals of what you say, and the relationship between you and your customers will change dramatically and permanently.

Discussion Questions

* How do you greet customers in your workplace? Do you call them by name?

* How well do you get to know your customers and their likes and dislikes?

* How do you thank people for their business?

· 8 ·

Murphy's Law Practice

Most people have heard of Murphy's Law—the principle that if something can go wrong, it probably will. At Murphy's Law Practice, a private legal firm on the outskirts of town, this principle was part of their heritage. It was a place where the toast always fell buttered side down, broken computers suddenly worked perfectly as soon as the repairman arrived, and personal injury lawyers regularly tripped over their own carpets.

This Monday morning was even more exciting than usual. A well-meaning but dim-witted temporary receptionist had misread the attendance chart last week and scheduled each of this week's clients with lawyers who were on vacation. As one person after another came to the office for their nonexistent appointments, the front lobby of the office was soon a cacophony of angry voices and deep sighs.

Around this time, Dr. Swami hobbled in to the office on a pair of crutches. A kindly man in Hindu garb, he was there to consult a lawyer after slipping and falling at an enlightenment retreat. As he approached the front desk, the lead receptionist gazed upon him with a look of annoyed resignation and uttered the same phrase that she had repeated that morning with the last twenty people: "Sir, your appointment isn't gonna happen today. The lawyer is on vacation."

He smiled serenely and replied, "Nothing in life is permanent."

The receptionist looked back with a glance of world-weariness and replied, "So do you want to reschedule?"

"I would like to help you achieve inner peace."

"We could all use more of that, mister," she sighed. Then, suddenly turning serious, she returned his gaze and said, "What do you have in mind?"

"Breathe deeply and visualize the client in your mind."

"Ugh . . . I see an angry person," she replied.

"No, no, no," he said with a polite chuckle. "You see a radiant, happy client. What are you telling this radiant, happy client?"

As Dr. Swami kept speaking, the other office staffers were soon gathered around the receptionist's desk listening in rapt attention. For once, here was a client who not only wasn't chewing them out, but was actually trying to help them. Before long, he had them all sitting in lotus positions on the floor as he had them visualize gracefully floating past their clients' anger, as they learned to say things designed to speak to their clients' interests and calm them down.

Soon everyone was chanting in unison things like, "I understand how you feel," "I will do everything I can to help make this better," and "Let's look at some alternatives to this problem." Then they opened their eyes and gazed at one another with a look of pleasant surprise. It was as though they had just found something very valuable. Dr. Swami rose and grabbed his crutches to leave.

The staff all gathered at the door and waved good-bye to Dr. Swami—and then grimaced in unison as he fell down the stairs onto the sidewalk. As he rose again and dusted himself off, he smiled and pointed to his temple, saying, "Remember, happy clients are all in your mind" as he hobbled off.

Moral: *Shine When Things Go Wrong*

There is one big problem with the idea that customer service is all about being "nice to people"—namely, the fact that most of us already come to work every morning planning to be nice to customers. But then things inevitably go wrong, people get upset and challenge us, and before we know it, we find that human nature takes over. When we are confronted, our natural urge is to defend ourselves, and so we act, well . . . defensively.

The key to handling tough situations is to learn how to speak to the other person's interest. Please note: This doesn't mean doing things you shouldn't do, or sacrificing your own self-respect. You don't have to give customers a refund that they aren't entitled to, for example, or acknowledge personal insults. What it does mean is that you learn to acknowledge that your customers are frustrated—or tell them that you will do your very best, or offer other face-saving alternatives. These options are a lot better than just saying, "I'm sorry sir, that's not our policy." Aren't they? Learn what to say when things go wrong, and you'll see an incredible change in the relationship between you and your customers.

Discussion Questions

✳ How can you practice "service recovery" when something goes wrong?

✳ What things can you say to make people feel better when there is a problem?

✳ What can your team do to manage stress in difficult customer situations?

· 9 ·

Chilly Willy

Penguins are chilly by nature. So when you have a bunch of them under contract to build an addition to your winter cottage, you shouldn't expect a barrel of laughs. But when John and Janet Smith came into town to inspect the work in progress on their vacation home, they still expected Penguin Construction to be civil and let them know how the project was going.

After they pulled into the driveway, they went up to the first penguin they saw. This penguin refused John's extended hand and snorted, "Willy's the boss—over there." A little miffed, they walked over to Willy, the construction crew chief, who greeted them gruffly and then sullenly followed them around as they looked over the details of the job.

As they walked around the job site, Janet pointed out a crack in the foundation, and Willy said nothing, nodding and taking a drag on his cigarette. A few minutes later, when John noticed a misaligned frame joint, Willy shrugged and kept moving. By the time they had looked over everything, John exclaimed, "There are a few

things that need to get fixed here." Turning away from them, Willy muttered "Yep," waddled off toward his truck, and drove away. Meanwhile, a few other penguins worked silently in the background, not acknowledging the Smiths, while others stood around in the far corner eating herrings from their lunch pails and laughing coarsely.

Things didn't go much better in the days and weeks that followed after the Smiths got back from the job site. Phone calls were not returned, progress reports were nonexistent, and the rude receptionist at Penguin Construction had seemingly no interest in being helpful. "That'll teach us to pick the lowest-priced contractor in the future," sighed Janet, as she hung up the phone from yet another fruitless attempt to get answers from them.

Finally the Smiths did get a reaction from Penguin Construction—when the penguins opened their mail one day and discovered that the Smiths had filed a breach-of-contract lawsuit. The penguins were flapping and squawking and making frantic attempts to contact the Smiths, who were now as silent as the penguins had been, responding to calls and letters with a terse, "Please talk to our lawyer."

In court, the Smiths laid out a carefully detailed case: the problems they had seen, the rudeness and indifference that greeted them when they visited the job site, and the lack of response afterward. When it was Willy's turn to take the stand, he looked down at the floor and muttered, "Hey, we were going to take care of all of this stuff."

The judge reached for her gavel. "But the record shows that you didn't bother to tell the Smiths any of that," she said. "Case decided in favor of the plaintiff."

Moral: *Silence Isn't Golden*

You may think that bad service is a matter of saying the wrong things to people. But sometimes it's a matter of not saying anything at all. In a customer situation, silence is often perceived as rudeness, and for most people a lack of response is one of the most disrespectful situations they encounter as customers.

You may get the silent treatment from anyone who serves the public, but professionals such as doctors, lawyers, and contractors are often the culprits, perhaps because they mistakenly believe that their expertise absolves them from the need to be responsive. And unfortunately, they often pay for this attitude. For example, emotional intelligence researcher and book author Daniel Goleman found that physicians who are perceived as having a poor "bedside manner" are substantially more likely to be sued for malpractice.

This doesn't mean that if you are naturally quiet and reserved, you suddenly need to become the life of the party around customers. We're all quite capable of delivering excellent service experiences with the personalities we were born with. But it does mean that we need to pay attention to what customers are saying, and then respond appropriately within the bounds of our personalities. Try being more proactive in your own feedback to customers, and see what a difference it makes!

Discussion Questions

✱ Do you have people who are rude or unresponsive working with your customers? How might you change this situation?

✱ Do customers have to contact you for the status of their issues, or do you proactively get in touch with them?

✱ How would you handle a situation where a customer wasn't happy with the way she was treated?

· 10 ·

Whatever

"This is going to be some wedding!" Chloe exclaimed, clutching her cell phone. "I've got people coming from three states to watch Mark and me get married. Oh, hold on just a minute. . . ." With her other hand on the keys of the cash register, she finished ringing up a woman's pair of pumps, wordlessly pushed the shoes and change at the customer, and went back to her conversation. "Now, let me tell you about what we're planning to have the bridesmaids wear. . . ."

Chloe had big plans for her life, and Smedley's Shoe Store wasn't exactly part of them. But for now, it was a job, especially while Mark finished up his last year at State Tech. She continued talking into the cell phone as the next customer came up to the register. "Do you know what my friend Jenny wants to wear to the wedding? Yeah, isn't that ridiculous? A purple dress? Give me a break!"

As she kept talking, this customer motioned to ask Chloe a question, and she cut him off by holding up a finger as she giggled at what her friend was saying on the phone. When she finally put the phone down and gave the customer a distant "Hello," he responded by saying,

"Young lady, shouldn't you be helping customers like me instead of yakking with your friends?"

Chloe tapped her foot and sighed "What-ever" audibly under her breath as she grudgingly helped him find a pair of Oxfords in his size, then rang up his purchase.

As he disappeared into the crowd of the mall, she picked up the phone again and recounted the whole episode to her friend. Looking at the receipt from his credit card, she sighed and said, "Who is this dork anyway? Let's see, Mr. M. Hatch—hmm, never heard of him. Anyway, we've got lots more to catch up on. . . ."

Soon another customer came over with a pair of sneakers, and as she picked up the box, she could feel it slip out of her hands and start tumbling to the floor. As she lunged to catch it, her finger jammed on the edge of the cash register—and by the time her shift ended an hour later, it was turning red and swelling up around her trapped engagement ring. Starting to get a little scared, she hopped into her little red subcompact and drove a half mile to the hospital emergency room.

At the hospital, sitting nervously on the edge of a cot behind a flimsy curtain, she waited for what seemed like an eternity before a white-coated doctor finally rushed in with a cell phone in his hand. With his back turned to her, he loudly debated with someone what the two of them should have for lunch tomorrow, and where they should play golf next week on their day off.

After a couple of minutes, Chloe finally raised her voice and asked the doctor, "Are you going to help me?"

"I guess, " he said lackadaisically, still not turning around to face her.

"And by the way, this ring is my engagement ring, so I really don't want anything to happen to it. Okay?" she continued.

"Whatever," replied the doctor, as he started to punch another number in on his cell phone.

"I don't think you're listening to me at all!" Chloe finally exclaimed.

"You're right," he said, finally turning around to face her.

"Hi . . . um . . . Doctor Hatch."

"Hi, Chloe," he replied, finally breaking into a smile. "Look, I couldn't resist having a little fun with you, but I really do care about your engagement ring. Let's see what we can do here." He applied a topical anesthetic and a lubricant cream, and after a couple of minutes the ring was finally wriggled free from her finger with no damage.

A few minutes later, as the doctor wrapped a bandage around her finger, Chloe felt relieved. Turning to the doctor, she said, "Thank you so much—I really appreciate you saving my ring and taking care of this sprain. Now, can you prescribe me anything?"

"Yes," he replied with a grin. Picking up a white prescription pad, he scribbled and handed it to her, as they both laughed. "All right, I definitely will follow this order, Dr. Hatch," she replied as she glanced at the words written in bold letters on the prescription: "Turn off your cell phone at work."

Moral: *Focus on Your Customer*

The phrase "You're here to work" sounds like the hallmark of the joyless workplace—even if there is a point to it. But let's turn this point around into something much more important for you and me: When you learn to keep your attention on your customers, you start developing interpersonal and leadership skills that will stick with you for the rest of your life.

Most of us start our careers in the same place—the bottom. But let's fast-forward through the years and look at whose careers are booming. Just look at the most successful people you know, or read the life stories of top business leaders, and see if you agree: The difference is often simply how engaged they were at filling customer needs in the most entry-level jobs. If you scratch the surface of any customer service position—even at the very bottom—you will find a free education on how to work with customers, and these lessons can often form the seeds of your own personal success.

Discussion Questions

* Does your workplace have a culture where the customer comes second? If so, why?

* What would you say to an employee who was just going through the motions of the job?

* How could you motivate people to care more about your workplace and your customers?

Section III
R-E-S-P-E-C-T

· 11 ·

The Knight Shift

One dank evening, Sir Gawain and King Arthur were sitting around the tap room in the basement of Arthur's castle, catching up on old times.

"So how goes it, your highness?" said Gawain heartily, as the king drew a tall pint of ale for his guest.

"Well, the situation with the peasants is a riot," sighed Arthur.

"They can be pretty funny sometimes," nodded Gawain.

"No, I mean *really* a riot. They aren't paying their taxes, and they constantly mass outside my castle with protest rallies. It's like they don't appreciate having a fiefdom to do subsistence farming on anymore."

"Sorry to hear that," Gawain said sympathetically. He paused for a moment and then continued. "So let me ask you a question, your highness. How well do you know the peasants on your lands?"

"Hardly at all," shot back the king. "Isn't that why we build moats?"

"I see," continued Gawain. "And what happens when these peasants have a complaint?"

He shrugged. "Well, off with their heads, of course."

Gawain smiled and nodded. "I think I see the problem, your highness. It sounds like it might be a job for my crew."

"Your crew?"

"Yes, of course. We're all knights. And from what you're describing, it sounds like you could use a little valor and chivalry out among the masses."

"Well, you're in luck," said the king, "because speaking of masses, there's a crowd of angry peasants outside the castle gates right now. Have fun."

Gawain tipped his hat and took his leave from the tap room— and then, thinking quickly, took a detour through the kitchen, emerging from the castle with a tray of pastries. Heading toward the mob of angry peasants, he held the tray aloft. "A gift to thee from the king," he declared, as the peasants gathered around him. A couple of them reached tentatively for the delicacies and sampled a few. Seeing that no harm came to them, the crowd then descended on Sir Gawain and quickly devoured the whole tray. Then they dispersed and headed back for their hovels, with satisfied but puzzled looks on their faces.

"They're all gone now," proclaimed Gawain as he returned to the tap room.

"Incredible," said the king. "I have never been able to break up these mobs before, even with ten armed men! Oh, and by the way, we're missing a tray of pastries I was about to offer you."

"Bloody mice . . . I have the same problem in my castle," replied Gawain. "You can't leave anything uncovered in the kitchen anymore these days. But as far as the peasants go, I think that all you really need is a little more chivalry."

"Yes, yes, you mentioned that word earlier," the king nodded. "Pray tell, what do you mean by it?"

Gawain smiled. "Chivalry is a code of conduct that all knights follow. Things like, Thou shalt defend all weaknesses. Thou shalt not lie. Be respectful of others, and avenge the wronged. It's kind of like what businesses in the larger fiefdoms refer to as their mission and vision statements."

King Arthur rolled his eyes. "So you are proposing treating a bunch of riotous peasants like some polite community service project?"

"Don't knock what you haven't tried, your highness. Of course, if you'd rather do it your way. . . ."

"No, no," interrupted the king. "I do, at least grudgingly, have to give you credit for breaking up the mob tonight. Well, then," he said as he rose to leave, "carry on, sir."

In the days and weeks that followed, Gawain and his knights were soon out among the populace, practicing their own brand of chivalry: bowing to the peasants, laying their capes across puddles for the ladies, and even letting the peasant children play peekaboo with their helmet visors. The knights helped clean and paint the neighborhood, too, using their steeds to haul people's trash away. Within a few weeks, Peasantville was starting to look more and more like Pleasantville.

In the meantime, some amazing things were starting to happen. First, the rallies outside the castle gates grew thinner and less vocal. Eventually, they stopped altogether. Then, one evening, a peasant tiptoed over to Gawain and pressed a few copper coins in the palm of his hand. "Paying me taxes," the peasant mumbled in a whisper. "Just don't tell anyone, alrighty?" Soon another followed . . . and another . . . until the kingdom's tax coffers were once again overflowing.

A few weeks later, a jubilant King Arthur gathered his entire court for a banquet to celebrate an end to the peasant insurrection. Standing up in front of the crowd, Arthur said proudly, "Sir Gawain hath taught us all a valuable lesson. Instead of just having oaths of fealty, we're going to have service standards from now on. And given how well that good Sir Gawain's experiment worked for us, he hath convinced me to set up a permanent knight shift here." Pointing to the circular table in the adjacent meeting room, the king continued, "And what the heck, let's call it the Round Table."

After everyone applauded, the king then turned to Sir Gawain at the table of honor. "I shall give you anything you desire," he proclaimed. "In addition to thy normal consulting fee, of course."

Gawain paused for a moment, smiled, and said, "Well, I wouldn't mind a couple of saddle bags of those delicious pastries from your kitchen. And," he paused, "perhaps an introduction to the cute lass who bakes them?" Shortly afterward, as he rode off toward his fiefdom with the young woman riding happily alongside, he thought to himself that chivalry really did have its advantages.

Moral: *Treat Customers with Respect*

When was the last time you walked into a store and were greeted with a sign that said "No refunds"? Or an exercise club that posted a laundry list of rules and regulations? Most of us depend on customers for our livelihood, but too often we present an image to them that says, "We don't trust you, and we don't particularly like you, either."

It isn't because we are mean, rude people; it is because all too often, we look at the world through our own eyes, instead of our customers' eyes. As the chivalrous knight in this story demonstrated, the best way to develop a positive, mutual relationship with your customers is by taking a good, hard look at your own policies—and the underlying values behind them. The guidelines that Sir Gawain mentioned—which, incidentally, are taken from an actual medieval code of chivalry—were the principles that guided their courtly behavior. In much the same way, your own procedures have a strong influence on how "courtly" your customers are treated—and as King Arthur discovered, an enlightened respect for your customers can dramatically change what happens between you and them.

Even when you must enforce rules, your success often depends on building good relationships with people. Let's look at the latter-day incarnation of medieval knights—today's modern police force. Of course, they are in the business of arresting people who cause trouble. But good police departments see themselves as having a strong community outreach role as well. In my hometown, local police—including the police chief—patrol the downtown shopping district in bright yellow Volkswagen Beetles instead of imposing police cars, and they make it a point to get to know people in the community. Similarly, some state troopers carry teddy bears in their patrol cars, to hand to scared children when they make traffic stops. Chivalry is still alive and well among many of the brave men and women who protect our safety, and with a little planning, it can be with you and your team as well. So, don't just be enforcers with customers—treat them as knights would, and watch your business soar!

Discussion Questions

✳ How could you and your team be more "knightly" with your own customer base?

✳ When customers are dissatisfied, what kinds of things could you do or say to make them feel respected?

✳ Do you have a written "code of conduct" that guides your actions with customers?

· **12** ·

Piggies

t was the day before Valentine's Day—traditionally one of the biggest sales days of the year at Piggy Truffles. And for the pigs who worked behind the counter, resplendent in their dark suits and bow ties, it also meant a crush of everyday creatures lining up to purchase their wares, instead of the carriage-trade customer base to which they'd grown accustomed. As Fauntleroy, the manager on duty that afternoon, put it, "It's like dealing with pigs at the trough."

The founders of Piggy Truffles, a group of swine who had gotten wealthy in the options market, carefully cultivated an image of elegance and exclusivity about their product. They considered themselves masters of making delicacies for the haute cuisine set, and advertised their business in the finest home and lifestyle magazines. But there was nothing elegant about the teeming hordes of customers crowding into their shop today, and the strain was starting to show on everyone.

Still, Fauntleroy did what he could to keep his line moving, as a middle-aged beaver made his way up to the front of the line with an opened box.

"These truffles don't taste very good. I think they're stale," said the beaver, with some visible annoyance.

"There is nothing finer than Piggy Truffles," Fauntleroy sniffed in response. "This isn't rotgut that anyone could buy down at Squeal-Mart. There is nothing wrong with our quality. Next, please."

As the beaver grabbed the box and stormed off, a hen came up to the counter, gingerly putting a small red purse in front of her with her right talon. "It would mean the world to my elderly mother to have some Piggy Truffles for Valentine's Day. Could you deliver a box overnight for me?"

"Tell her that if she wants Piggy Truffles for Valentine's Day, she needs to plan ahead. Next, please."

A young weasel shuffled up next, clutching a small number of bills in his paw. "I wanna get my sister some of your truffles, mister, but I only have a few dollars. Do you have anything on sale that I could buy her?"

"Piggy Truffles simply aren't for everyone. Next, please."

Finally a tall, lanky horse strode up and stared angrily across the counter. "I'm here to complain," he said.

"Oh dear, dear," replied Fauntleroy with mock sincerity. "Whatever could be the matter?"

"I've been standing in line here and listening to you guys and, well, for starters . . . you're behaving like a bunch of pigs."

"My dear horse," Fauntleroy said indignantly, "we *are* a bunch of pigs."

"Yeah, and you're all too busy with your snouts in the air to do things like listen to any of your customers," said the horse. Speaking sarcastically and affecting an elegant accent, he added, "That's why the several thousand dollars I was about to spend on truffles for corporate gifts are now going to get spent on the finest foods that *other* providers have to offer." With that, he turned on his tail and left—to thundering applause from everyone else waiting in line. A good number of other customers turned around and exited right behind him.

That hurt—because the pigs all knew that by losing that much business, they would be missing out on bonuses from corporate headquarters that would have been almost as fat as they were. But indirectly, it may have saved their bacon in the long term. As the next group of customers approached—a rowdy bunch of young whooping cranes—Fauntleroy greeted them with a big smile and said heartily, "Glad you're here, folks! Can I offer you a sample of some of these fine truffles?"

Moral: *Good Products Don't Excuse Bad Service*

Some companies—and some people—follow an all-too-familiar path once they become successful with their products or services. They let success morph into exclusivity, which eventually turns into arrogance and hubris, which ultimately leads to failure. You notice it when a shop closes two hours before most people get off from work, or when a restaurant has a big fat sign reading "No substitutions" over the front counter, or when people act like it's all about them rather than the customer.

Do people develop such attitudes because they are mean-spirited or rude? Ironically, probably not. More likely, it is an accumulation of small situations—the customer who demands too much, the person who tries to abuse a return policy, or the novice who takes up too much of our time. In response, we make too many rules with too little flexibility, and eventually we develop an attitude that seems like contempt for our customers.

In time, we can even forget what it was like when we were hungry for everyone's business and wanted to please them. So pay attention to these little frustrations—especially when you are very good at what you do—and remember that great service always starts with a fundamental respect for your customers as fellow human beings.

Discussion Questions

❋ Have you ever seen a case where superiority gets mistaken for excellence?

❋ How can you help keep people from reacting dismissively to customer demands?

❋ Do peak periods bring out the worst in your team? Is there anything you can do to help boost morale during times like these?

· **13** ·

The Bee Line

"**D**o bees play with one another?" Cindy asked, wide-eyed, as her father Ed tended to the hives that their family kept in the backyard.

"Bees are stupid," he snorted. "They do everything by sense of smell. If you mix two colonies of bees, they'll fight each other to the death—just because they smell different."

"So bees can never be friends with other bees, Daddy?"

"Well, there is one way you can mix 'em. You put a piece of newspaper between two colonies in a box." Ed smiled as he slid the last hive back in. "By the time the bees eat their way through the newspaper, their smells have mixed enough that they can get along with one another."

"Oh . . . cooool," said Cindy thoughtfully.

"And speaking of letting the bees play, it's time for me to stop playing and get back to work. Want to come into the store with me, Cindy?"

"Yes, Daddy!" Cindy squealed as she jumped up and down. She loved going into her father's convenience store. It had comic books to read, cold soda pop to drink, and lots of interesting people coming and going. Soon she was curled up comfortably behind the counter as their first customer of the day, a middle-aged man wearing a turban, walked through the door.

"Drat . . . another one of those foreigners," Ed whispered to his daughter. "Some of these people can barely speak English, and they're always trying to haggle for a better deal." Soon the man in the turban came up to the counter with a Sunday paper and some snacks in his hand, and politely made his purchase. He smiled and nodded at Cindy, then turned to leave as she waved back at him.

Next, an elderly woman with a walker hobbled slowly toward the back of the store. "Old fogy," Ed intoned quietly. "These geezers take forever to shop, they're always blocking the aisles, and they never have money for anything." A couple of minutes later, the old woman came up to the front counter to purchase a smart-looking umbrella and stopped to pat Cindy on the head as she headed out the door.

A few minutes later, a gang of teenagers strutted in, wearing baggy shorts and showing off dance moves to one another as they passed around a digital music player. "Boy . . . more teenagers," sighed Ed. "These punks will steal us blind if we don't keep a sharp eye on them." Moments later, the teens all came to the counter with cold Cokes and fistfuls of candy bars. As they were paying, they all cracked up as Cindy started to imitate some of their dance moves. A couple of them gave her a big thumbs-up on their way out.

Ed exhaled deeply as the teens left the store, and then he said under his breath, "Sometimes I wonder whatever happened to the good customers these days. You know, normal people who aren't a problem." Then he smiled and turned to his daughter. "Oh, by the way, I need to duck in the back to restock the soda pop. Holler if a customer comes in, okay, honey?"

"Okay, Daddy!" Cindy giggled and nodded.

A few minutes later, when Ed emerged from the stockroom, he found his way was blocked. The doorway was covered with sheets of newspaper. And little Cindy was on tiptoes, stretching to the top of her four-foot frame, taping more sheets to the sides of the door.

Ed looked down at his daughter from over the top of this newspaper barricade. "Now *what* is going on here, young lady?"

"Well," she said as she looked up at him angelically. "You said that bees can be friends if they break through a newspaper. So I was putting one between you and those other people in the store."

"Huh?"

". . . I figgered by the time you and the other people busted through the paper, you'd be friends again. Cuz' you'd all smell the same."

"Ah, now I see," replied Ed, thinking back to the people who had just come in his store. "It's about those other customers."

"I *like* those people, Daddy. Those people wit' the funny hats, an' the old fogeys, an' even the punks who dance around. I wanna be friends with all of 'em."

"Well, guess what," said Ed, as he ripped through the paper with a karate chop of his hand and scooped up his daughter in his arms. "Looks like I do, too."

Moral: *Respect Diversity*

Colonies of bees actually do behave the way that they are described in this story. For them, it is a survival instinct that helps protect their food supply from outsiders. Similarly, many other animals instinctively reject animals of the same species that are "different" from themselves, to keep weaker animals from interfering with the hunt for food.

As humans, we have perhaps inherited the same animal tendency to be suspicious of anyone who looks or acts too "different" from us—yet nowadays, discrimination serves no useful purpose for us other than to take away the legitimate rights of other human beings.

Sadly, we are not that far removed from a time when people were denied service because of their religion, skin color, or gender. While such overt discrimination is much more unfashionable nowadays—not to mention illegal—more subtle forms of it still exist. By learning to respect all of our customers, we not only do the right thing, but greatly enrich our life experience.

Discussion Questions

* Do people treat different kinds of customers differently at your workplace?

* What would you do if someone was stereotyping customers because of their race, ethnicity, age, or gender?

* What can you do to help people understand and respect diversity?

· 14 ·

Going to the Dogs

Two dogs were sitting next to each other at obedience school, catching up on things while their owners chatted in the corner.

"So, what do you think of this class so far, Brutus?"

"Oh, you know, the usual, Fifi. In fact, I was just thinking . . . hey, wait, look over there. Here comes a mailman! Woof! Woof!"

As he lunged toward the door, the firm voice of his owner rang across the room. "*Sit*, Brutus!" Before he even knew it, he was sitting crouched on his hind legs—growling in frustration, but sitting nonetheless. After his owner went back to his conversation, he trudged back to Fifi and plopped himself down.

"You wonder why we keep following these orders—even though our teeth are sharper than people's?" she whispered in his ear.

"Because we'll do anything for doggie treats," Brutus sighed. "And in time, it just gets to be a habit, you know?"

"Yeah," replied Fifi. "After a while, you simply get used to the fact that when they tell you to sit, you sit."

"Tell me about it," Brutus exclaimed. "Just once, I'd like to see my owners go to the kitchen for a snack and have someone hold it two feet over their heads, saying, 'Here, beg!' "

Fifi nodded in agreement, and then gestured toward the rest of the class. "You know, the instructor was talking about something called 'reinforcement' with the owners. She was saying that when you reward the behavior you want, you get more of it."

"Hmm." smiled Brutus. "Reinforcement. You might be on to something there—I've got an idea. . . ."

· · ·

A week later, back in class again, Brutus came over to Fifi, his tail wagging excitedly. "It works!" he exclaimed.

"What works?" asked Fifi, a quizzical look on her face.

"That reinforcement stuff. I've got my owners trained really well now," he replied. "Tell me, Fifi, what did you have for dinner tonight?"

"Well, dog food, as always," sighed Fifi.

"That's my point. When my owners are having steak for dinner, I bring over their evening newspaper and then nuzzle my face in their lap. They love it—and before you know it, I'm eating the same porterhouse they are."

"You're kidding," replied Fifi, suddenly becoming interested. "That's so cool!"

"And that's just the beginning. I've been starting to train them in other things lately, and now they even come when I call them. Next week, I'm going to try and get them to sit!"

"Wow . . . I've got to try that," she exclaimed.

"And you know, if these humans who are in business could only figure out how to do the same thing with their customers, they could make a mint! If they just started complimenting people and playing up to their needs, most of them would probably get more business than they could handle."

"You've got a good point there, Brutus . . . er . . . Brutus?" As she finished, Fifi looked up to see him hurtling toward the approaching silhouette of the mailman at the door, as his owner yelled, "*Sit,* Brutus!"

Moral: *Use Positive Reinforcement*

Legendary sales trainer and motivational speaker Zig Ziglar once said, "You can have everything in life you want, if you will just help enough other people get what they want." If you deal with customers, the art of positive reinforcement is one of the quickest ways to make this statement come true in your own work. People buy more, complain less, and cooperate better with people who find ways to make them feel good.

Virtually any encounter with a customer can become fertile ground for practicing positive reinforcement. Of course, there are obvious ways to stroke your customers, such as asking them what they like, complimenting them on their tastes, or doing them favors. But at a more subtle level, even more difficult situations can provide opportunities for positive reinforcement— for example:

- When a customer is unhappy about something, you empathize with her feelings.

- When a novice is struggling with a new product, you commend him on how hard he is trying.

- When things have gone wrong, you do something extra for your customers to help them feel better.

Perhaps the key to giving customers positive reinforcement is realizing that they are not just part of a faceless stream of oil changes, doctor's appointments, or retail purchases; they are people like you, with likes, dislikes, and feelings. When you learn to tap into these human emotions and help customers feel good, the rewards will come back to you many times over.

Discussion Questions

❋ How well do you understand the motivations of your customers?

❋ Can you think of new ways to make people want to do business with you?

❋ What kinds of things can you do to encourage more of the customer behaviors you want?

Section IV
Service Strategy

· 15 ·

Shrink to Fit

I t was certainly tough times when they closed down the state mental health facility, but when a group of laid-off psychologists decided to start a local bar and grill, they had high hopes that their lofty degrees and expertise in human behavior would translate into a crowded drinking establishment. "Just different kinds of counseling and medications this time," joked one of the partners, as he helped everyone set up the tables and light fixtures.

But soon after The Freudian Slip opened for business, it was clear that something wasn't quite right. Ed, the young dishwasher they hired, was one of the first to notice that something was unusual about this place. He had knocked around the restaurant and hospitality business for years, and the kinds of things he was hearing from behind the bar were different from anything he had ever heard before, things like:

> "I see that she wouldn't let you buy her a drink. Tell me how you are feeling."

"Watching the home team lose this game must be very upsetting for you."

"We need to assess whether you have had too much to drink. What does this inkblot look like to you?"

"It sounds like you are working through some emotions about paying this check."

Then one of the patrons at the bar pulled Ed aside and said glumly, "Once upon a time the bartender was my therapist. Now my therapist is the bartender. It's not the same." That's when Ed knew he had to speak up. Politely, he went over to one of the owners and said, "Doc, I don't think that guy on the end is having a good time."

"I think that this customer is still having conflicts with his mother," he replied stiffly.

"I disagree, Doc," said Ed. "For most people, their idea of a great night out isn't hanging around a bunch of shrinks. Something has to change here."

Eventually, the owners decided to do what everyone did in their former profession—get help. Ed started taking the psychologists around to other bars in the area and pointed out the things that bartenders and wait staff did to make people feel at home, as they all furtively took notes. Later, he brought in his friends from the restaurant business to talk frankly about why people went to bars and how they wanted to watch sports, find companionship, and meet the opposite sex. Perhaps most important, Ed got everyone to agree to stop meeting downstairs every Thursday to have a primal scream therapy session "for old time's sake," because the loud shrieks were upsetting the patrons.

There were rough spots at first. For example, a week later, Dr. Smith tried to practice his sports banter by asking one patron, "What would it mean to you if the Dallas Cowboys won this game?" But soon they all learned to loosen up. They started calling people by their names, and they even got comfortable with a little small talk as they served up drinks and snacks. A name change for the business followed, and in time, the new Liquid Therapy started to feel more like a real neighborhood bar and less like a managed-care counseling session.

They shifted gears from trying to "facilitate" discussions with patrons to hosting sing-alongs around an old upright piano. They eventually found that they could have real one-on-one conversations with people without constantly validating their feelings. And in time, about the only nod to their former profession was when they invited a sports psychologist to pick apart the opposing football team's strategy on game days.

There were still moments, of course, when they relapsed. Like the time a man came up to the bar saying that he was having a bad day, and everyone behind the counter instinctively blurted out, "Tell me what you are feeling," instead of the agreed-upon, "Can I get you a cold beer?" But soon the crowds started coming back, again and again—and everyone agreed that this change was truly therapeutic, in the most important sense of the word.

Moral: *Get Into Your Customers' Heads*

Here is a quick thirty-second lesson on how to keep more customers than anyone else: Learn what these customers like, and find ways to give it to them.

Many businesses—particularly small ones—focus on themselves. The store whose advertising talks about what "we" sell, and not how the merchandise can benefit "you." The consultant who talks about what "I" do instead of what "you" need. The gift shop that greets its customers with a big sign that says "You break it, you've bought it." And employees aren't immune to this condition, either: The store clerk who greets you with "We're closing in five minutes" has yet to learn a critical success trait that will improve her life and career.

The psychologists in our story had to make a critical shift when they started running a bar—namely, they had to forget about their own lofty credentials and start asking what bar patrons wanted. In real life, we need to examine everything we do from the same perspective: Who are my customers, and what do they want and need? If you look critically at many of the world's most successful businesses, you can often trace their success to getting to know their customers, taking one thing that these customers wanted or needed, and then doing it better than anyone else. The same approach is one of the quickest ways to build your own personal success. Try it today, and watch the great things that happen.

Discussion Questions

* Have you ever seen any real-life examples of people focusing on their expertise versus customer needs?

* How could you learn more about what things turn your customers on or off?

* Are there people in your organization who can help you see things through your customers' eyes?

· 16 ·

Sloth Is Not a Vice

Once upon a time, deep in the jungle, a small company called Huts to You made thatched straw huts for people to live in. They made the best homes around, and people came from far and wide to buy their huts. But they had a problem.

Their problem wasn't sales. Nor was it expenses. Their biggest problem was sloth. Or, to be more accurate, sloths. Like most jungle businesses, Huts to You had a lot of three-toed sloths on the payroll, because they were far and away the most common mammal around. Problem is, when you hire animals that ordinarily hang upside down in trees and take an entire week to digest a meal, it creates a whole new kind of productivity challenge.

And so the situation led to the same problem, week after week. Customers would place an order for their huts. Then they would come back a week later, only to find some sloth slowly and methodically putting individual pieces of straw on their barely started home. It bothered Huts to You management that customers were upset when their orders were delayed, but at the same time the managers were realistic enough to know that the alternative would be a serious labor shortage.

Finally, management decided to take action. Soon the sloths were gathered together in a focus group, hanging upside down from a palm tree overhead, as the managers sat at a conference table below them. A perky facilitator stood up, thrust her arms skyward toward the hanging sloths, and chirped, "What are some of the things that make it great to work with sloths?"

After an interminable pause, the answers started coming slowly from the sloths, in their usual gravelly monotone.

"Uh . . . we do a good job."

"Yeah, in fact, we do a better job than most animals."

"We just do it more slowly than others."

"Besides, we hang around here constantly."

"And you get to pay us in palm leaves."

As the last sloth finished speaking, the president and vice president looked at each other—and suddenly, a flash of insight crossed between them. The VP silently mouthed, "Slow as a selling point?" as the president nodded excitedly in agreement. They then turned back to the sloths and saw that they were all now fast asleep. But no matter—they had the answer!

Soon afterward, a young couple stopped by Huts to You wanting to purchase their first home. The manager looked at them and said, "I could probably have another animal handle your order in a week or two. But if we can work things out for you, I might actually be able to have a *sloth* do it."

The husband replied, "A sloth?" They looked at the manager quizzically as he continued. "Yes, sir, a sloth! I'm not sure if you are aware of this, but sloth-built homes are the finest that money can buy. Instead of rushing things, they spend weeks and weeks lavishing attention on your hut, working slowly and meticulously to produce the finest quality we can build. That's why only the most exclusive homes

in this part of the jungle have been produced by sloths. Of course, there is a waiting list . . ."

As he continued on, the man and his wife turned to each other, and then said excitedly, "Gosh, we want our house built by a sloth!" And six months later, when they finally moved in, they could hardly contain themselves, bringing in all of their family and friends to show off their new sloth-built home.

Soon, customers were coming from all around to demand real sloth-built homes from Huts to You, and they could barely keep up with the demand—which, ironically, was a good thing, since many customers now saw it as bragging rights that their homes were built as slowly as possible. And as for the sloths themselves, it was a welcome change to go from being laggards to slow, lumbering celebrities. As one of them recently put it, "People are finally learning that the finest things take time."

Moral: *Undercommit and Overdeliver*

Do you think that customer satisfaction just depends on your product or service? If so, then consider these facts:

- According to Bill Rose of the Service & Support Professionals Association, nearly two-thirds of calls placed to call centers are simply to check on the status of an existing problem. Therefore, setting better expectations about when a problem will be resolved translates into fewer calls and fewer complaints.

- Paul Greenberg, a consultant and expert in customer relationship management (CRM), has noted a university study that shows that customers will stick around—even when their customer satisfaction is low—if they have high expectations for the future.

• Makers of numerous products, ranging from ice cream to custom homes, have built lucrative markets for themselves by creating premium products where none had existed before—in other words, they cashed in by exceeding people's expectations.

What does all of this mean in layman's terms? It means that setting expectations is one of the most critical aspects of keeping customers happy. It is a skill that has three components: 1) giving people a realistic sense of what to expect, 2) selling the benefits of what you do, and then 3) consistently exceeding these expectations. When you do a good job of setting expectations, you make it much easier to play to your strengths and be successful with customers.

Discussion Questions

∗ What can you do to set appropriate and realistic customer expectations?

∗ Are there hidden "selling points" you could be promoting to your customers?

∗ How could you make the best use of the resources you have to create good customer experiences?

· 17 ·

The Mopes

he Mopes were a once-proud people who had sadly fallen on hard times in recent years. The reason? Their approach to customer service was the same as their approach to everything in life: They moped.

There was no question in anyone's mind about the contributions the Mopes had made to civilization, such as dark, brooding novels and deep intellectual films. Not to mention their role in coining a phrase heard around the world: To "mope" about something meant to, well, act like a typical Mope.

But these days, it was getting harder and harder to eke out a living as a full-time Mope.

Back in the old days, getting jobs and keeping customers wasn't such a problem, because it seemed as if everyone acted like Mopes. Indeed, retail stores, public utilities, medical practices, and government offices were once hotbeds of Mopes in the not-too-distant past. But times had changed, and in a world of service standards, customer skills training, and big-box stores with perky greeters, many of the Mopes found themselves and their dull, leaden manner left out in the cold.

In what had become a remarkably chipper world, the Mopes tried many things to get their customers back. For example, they tried putting more caffeine in their already-strong, dark coffee, but that only made them seem cranky and whiny. A later move to replace their somber, dark threads with more brightly colored clothing was quickly scrapped, after people joked about them looking like "Franz Kafka in business casual." Finally, some of them even went through a dreaded "smile training" program—and in many cases, their faces cracked.

Finally, in desperation, they visited a wise old man who lived high on a mountaintop. As the last of them filed somberly into his cave, the wise man looked up from his organic tea and said, "Welcome, my friends. You have traveled a great distance to see me. Tell me what it is that you seek."

"Being dour and serious just isn't the way it used to be," intoned one of them gravely. "Everyone wants people to be cheerful and upbeat these days. But it just isn't us. We have a long tradition of moping around."

"It sounds like this has been really hard for you," the wise man responded kindly.

"Yes, indeed! We practically invented searching for the meaning of life, but we don't know what ours is anymore," the Mope replied.

Another Mope chimed in: "Yeah, cracking smiles and saying 'We're delighted to serve you' isn't only out of character for us—it threatens our culture."

The wise man looked around the room, gazed lovingly at them, smiled, and said, "Play to your strengths." Then he disappeared.

• • •

When the Mopes returned from the mountaintop, several of them gathered in the parlor of a grim-looking Victorian house, engaging in one of their favorite pastimes—listening to selections from their five CD set of "Love Songs for the Brokenhearted"—as they discussed the wise man's advice.

First, one of them broke the ponderous silence by saying, "This man told us to play to our strengths. But look, we're all Mopes. What kind of strengths could we possibly have in today's world?"

"Well, let's talk about who we are, and see if there are any strengths there," said another.

"Well, for starters, we don't say very much," said the group's leader.

"That means we could be good listeners!"

"We complain all the time," continued the leader.

"That means we could be great critical thinkers!" replied another.

"We are constantly wrapped up in ourselves," the leader intoned.

Catching on, several Mopes in the group murmured in unison, "That means we could understand other people better than most!"

And so the discussion went. As new strengths were revealed, new career paths emerged. By evening's end, their direction was clear.

Soon afterward, the Mopes seemed to have a whole new lease on life—as art historians who slowly and painstakingly described the intricacies of Ming Dynasty vases; as psychotherapists who sat patiently with their clients and said, "Umm-hmm, please tell me more"; and as high school English teachers who were all too willing to go over, one more time, how to diagram a sentence.

Word spread quickly about their cultural rebirth, and eventually—although they would never, ever phrase it this way—it was good to be a Mope again.

Moral: *You Don't Have to Be Perky to Give Great Service*

There is a customer service myth that the best service is provided by perky, happy, outgoing people who typify the "service personality." Unfortunately, this myth reaches the highest levels of the customer-service profession.

The problem is, not everyone reacts well to an overdose of "chipper." In fact, according to psychologists, nearly 40 percent of us prefer to play things straight and get to the point. Even worse, it leads people who don't naturally have an incandescent 100-watt grin and a ready quip to think that they aren't fit to work in service positions. In reality, nothing could be further from the truth.

Real service quality lies in connecting with other people and meeting their needs—no matter what your personality is. In my experience managing large-scale customer support operations, with the right skills and training, every kind of personality is capable of providing truly excellent service—even if you are a Mope. So be true to who you are, and use your own unique strengths to be a service star on your own terms.

Discussion Questions

* Do you welcome a diverse range of personalities on your service team?

* How can you help your less-outgoing people create great service?

* Do you take steps to create a good service experience for different customer personalities?

· **18** ·

By a Hare

Nature is all about adapting to your strengths. So, when a group of rabbits banded together to form an express delivery service, it made perfect sense. When other animals needed a package delivered, *Sproing!* Off hopped a cotton-tailed courier, package in paw. Soon, business was multiplying faster than the rabbits themselves, and the phrase "Send it by rabbit" had become a standard figure of speech among busy animals everywhere.

One sunny afternoon, a hedgehog named Suzy came into Rabbit Express with an important parcel—an antique family portrait carefully packaged in a sturdy shipping box. A burly, unshaven hare in a grease-stained uniform lumbered up to the counter. "Whaddya want, ma'am?"

"I'd like to send this package to my family over in East Meadow," Suzy said expectantly. "It's for a family reunion this weekend."

Scanning the address quickly, the hare replied, "Sorry, ma'am. Out of our delivery zone. Nuttin' we can do," as he tossed the package to the side.

"But only by a few blocks!" she wailed. "And this package is really important. Isn't there anything you can do for me?"

The hare shrugged without even looking back as he ambled back through the double doors into the warehouse, as she stood there, a tear welling in one corner of her eye.

Another animal standing behind her overheard this exchange and came over to her. "I have an idea. My friends and I could probably get the package there. It would take an extra day, but . . ."

"Oh, could you?" she exclaimed.

• • •

Not only did Suzy's package get delivered that week, but she and her family were so happy about how they were treated that they started asking the same animals to deliver more packages for them. Before long, their families and friends were doing the same. Corporate clients followed, and by the time a year had gone by, they were a full-fledged company whose personal service and lower rates led them to grow tremendously—to the point where they eventually became even bigger than their faster brethren at Rabbit Express.

At a gala dinner to celebrate their success, the company president—who had also been the one who originally offered to deliver Suzy's package—smiled at the podium as he finished recounting the story of how they got started. "You know, for a bunch of tortoises, I would have never expected any of us to get this far." Patting one of his colleagues on the shell, he continued, "But as I always used to say, slow and steady often wins the race."

Moral: *Go the Extra Mile*

This fictional story zeroes in on the two reasons most businesses lose their customers: They fail to give them what they want, and develop a rude "that's our policy" attitude about it.

Much like the tortoises in our story, many firms began—and prospered—by giving customers more than they expect, and making that standard part of their core values. Scratch the surface of many of the world's most successful companies and you will find an ingrained culture of going the extra mile. For example, employees of Nordstrom, the upscale department store, have been known to go to other stores to find customers something that was out of stock. Nordstrom has grown to become a nearly $8 billion company whose profits increased by more than 40 percent between 2004 and 2006.

In customer service, going above and beyond may be the single most valuable thing that you can do for your own career, for your team's success, and for your business's bottom line.

Discussion Questions

❋ What things can you do to go the extra mile for your customers?

❋ Are there areas where you can capitalize on a competitor's poor service?

❋ Does your service create word-of-mouth growth in your customer base?

Section V
You and Your Service Team

· 19 ·

Can I Help You?

As a customer admiringly held a beautiful crystal decanter in her hands, Sarah approached her with a welcoming smile on her face. "May I help you?" she said sweetly.

"It's *can* I help you!" a loud voice suddenly barked from the back room. "We always say *can* I help you when a customer comes in Grindle's Gift Shoppe." Sheepishly, Sarah said, "I'm sorry, Mr. Grindle," as she turned her attention back to the customer.

Long ago, Mr. Grindle became fed up with the kind of service he was seeing from his employees, who were mostly young people. Recently, he decided to do something about it. Compared with most retailers, he had lots and lots of rules about what to say to customers, how to ring up purchases, how to shelve the merchandise, and many other things. All of them had to be followed to the letter, or else his staff would get an earful, no matter who else was around. The way Grindle saw it, the only way to keep these entry-level types in line was to lay down the law.

When Sarah turned in her notice a few days later, he didn't really pay attention. "Stupid kids," he groused to himself. "No loyalty to keeping a job anymore. Probably got a new boyfriend or something." But she was the third person to leave in less than a month—and worse, he was still getting customer complaints, especially about how people were being treated when he wasn't personally in the shop. So he knew that something had to be done.

After his usual breakfast of prunes and raisin bran the next morning, Mr. Grindle decided that the problem was really simple: People still didn't have enough discipline. So that morning he drafted a memo in bold type, with large letters, and posted it on the back of the stockroom door for everyone to see. It read:

We Have to Follow the Rules of This Store!
All of Them—No Exceptions!
And We Have to Treat Our Customers Even Better!
More Rules Are Coming!
I Will Be Watching!

—THE MANAGEMENT OF GRINDLE'S GIFT SHOPPE

After this memo was posted, he could hear a little grumbling from some of his regular employees, just out of earshot. "Let 'em complain," thought Grindle. "No wonder no one's gotten a raise here in the last two years. Maybe now they'll get the message."

A couple of days later, Mr. Grindle came in to work and clicked shut the stockroom door behind him. As he walked briskly toward the double doors leading to the showroom floor, he could clearly make out a cracked, high-pitched voice saying, "Can I help you?" While he couldn't quite place who was speaking, he muttered to himself, "Someone's finally getting it right around here!" Then, as he stepped out onto the floor, he saw a bird circling overhead—a sleek, dark-plumed mynah bird, cackling, "Can I help you?" over and over.

He turned around to find an empty bird cage and a man in a delivery uniform from the local pet center. The delivery man had a look of amused bewilderment on his face, and before turning to leave, he looked at Grindle, shrugged, and said, "A present from your employees, sir."

Moral: *You Can't Create Good Service with Rules*

Rules have their place. They can help set standards, and they may deter people from stealing your toilet paper. But be careful what you wish for. Depending on rules to create your service quality is a little like depending on prisons to create great communities.

The reality is that truly great service springs from people who believe in what you are doing and enjoy coming to work each morning. Top companies know this. Southwest Airlines—the most consistently profitable airline in America—has an internal motto: "The customer comes second." Southwest has a long tradition of promoting teamwork and a sense of fun on the job—two key factors in its impressive history of high customer satisfaction ratings. The airline even insists on capitalizing the word "Employee" in all of its official communications.

Trying to create higher customer standards by bearing down on your employees is sometimes known as "kissing up and kicking down." Instead, start treating employees as your most important customers and see how it affects your "other" customers' satisfaction levels.

Discussion Questions

* Do any people in your organization try to "punish their way" to good service?

* Do you critically examine the reasons for turnover among your service team?

* Do people on your team buy in to your service procedures? If not, why not?

· 20 ·

The Coach

t was the first week on the job for "Sarge" Davis, and already things weren't going well.

Over the past thirty-five years, Sarge had been the most successful coach in the history of the local high school. They were state champions three times, and one of his teams became the only undefeated team in conference history. When it came time to retire from the school district, a kindly alumni booster helped him get a job managing a local chain grocery store.

But Sarge soon found that acting like a football coach was a bad idea in a grocery store. Telling people to "get their butts out on the field" led to puzzled stares from the cashiers in the break room. The old-timers unloading delivery trucks in the stockroom didn't want to hear lectures on "sweating the fundamentals." Even a lighthearted attempt to "go long" throwing a frozen turkey to one of the stock clerks backfired, as it slipped through his hands and shattered the plate glass in front of the deli counter.

The last straw came when, after getting several customer complaints, he made a lunchtime motivational speech to everyone about "putting on their game face." A couple of hours later, walking down the produce aisle, he noticed that several ripe melons had goofy faces drawn on them with marking pens, with the words "game face" scrawled underneath. As he thumped his knuckles on one of the melons in frustration, he knew that something was going to have to change.

Meanwhile, a neatly dressed young man walked over to him. "Hi, Coach! Got a minute to talk?"

"Sure . . . um, by the way, who are you?" he asked quizzically.

"My name is Joe," he replied, extending his hand. "The guy who manages the discount store next door. A lot of my employees are friends with your employees, and they all talk. Now, from what I hear, I think you may benefit from a little coaching yourself."

"Okay, then, Joe. Come on over to my office and let's chat."

As they settled down in his small office, Sarge spoke first. "You know, Joe, I really don't get it. On the football team, whatever I said went. And if someone wasn't performing, I'd get in their face and they'd get moving again. That's why we won games. Why are things so different in this store?"

Joe smiled, "Because your football players had a built-in motivation—to play in front of hundreds of fans, and maybe get into a good college program. Here at the store, you need to motivate people, not just bark out orders."

"Heck, back in the day when I worked, that's how bosses always treated me!" argued Sarge.

"Yeah, and dentists used to pull teeth without anesthetics," shot back Joe. "Times change, Sarge."

"All right then, Joe, I'm all ears," Sarge replied with a weary sigh.

"I guess that things couldn't get much worse than this past week. What would you do if you were in my shoes?"

"For starters, lose the whistle around your neck."

"Oh . . . yeah . . . you've got a point there," he said sheepishly, putting the whistle in his shirt pocket.

• • •

Over the next few days and weeks, Joe and Sarge met for lunch and talked about how coaches today need to be strategists and not just taskmasters. Sarge turned out to be a good pupil as well as a good coach. In time, he found himself changing his style to fit the rhythm of the retail business—encouraging people, stopping to talk to them about their strengths and career aspirations, and learning the ropes himself so that he could positively coach young employees on the mechanics of their jobs.

His efforts eventually led to a real change in attitude among the people on his team, which in turn led to happier customers and better performance. Perhaps the watershed moment came three months later, when on Boss's Day, the store employees surprised him with a cake inscribed "To Our Favorite Coach" and a plaque containing a shiny gold-plated whistle.

Sarge beamed, and as everyone applauded, a voice rose from the crowd of employees—"Here, Sarge, catch!" A frozen turkey hurtled toward his outstretched arms. As the turkey slipped through his hands and shattered the just-replaced plate glass in the deli counter, Sarge smiled and shrugged. He was finally home.

Moral: *Motivation Is All About Them, Not Just You*

Once upon a time, the stereotypical athletic coach—and the stereotypical manager—was a tough-love type who motivated through fear and intimidation.

Look at today's most successful coaches—like baseball's Joe Torre or basketball's Phil Jackson—and you'll see people who behave more like psychologists than slave drivers. Torre rarely raises his voice and is known for having hundreds of one-on-one meetings with team members, while Jackson quotes Zen principles and stresses teamwork. Both have one thing in common: more championships than anyone in their generation.

If you supervise others, take a hard look at your own coaching style. People hate being criticized, but love learning new skills. And when you put the basics of positive, strength-based coaching to work for you, you'll notice the difference in your team's performance.

Discussion Questions

* Does your own coaching style motivate people to excel?

* How can you encourage people for giving their best efforts?

* In what ways do you help people directly benefit from creating excellent service?

Epilogue:
Good Service Is More Than a Fable

Y ou have just finished reading a book of funny stories. But in the process, you have also taken a very powerful short course on human relations—a course with serious benefits for you and your career, as well as your customers. In closing, I'd like to invite you to look a little deeper into the lessons behind these humorous situations, and use them to create an entirely new level of success in your life.

While almost no one wants to hear a lecture on how to behave, most of us love learning new skills. That is why many of us don't benefit as much as we could from typical customer service training, particularly when the focus is on how to be "nice." When it comes to handling real-life customer situations, success is often the result of learning new skills—many of which go against our human nature.

In this book, the intention is to give you a fresh look at customer situations, through the lens of these new skills. In the process, we used the classic structure of works such as Aesop's Fables, as well as a powerful principle from behavioral psychology known as *modeling*. The essence of modeling is that when someone tells *us* how to behave, we tend to tune it out; but when we observe *others,* we learn from their behavior. In other words, as we read the story of how a pack of hyenas or a group of unemployed clowns handle their customer situations, and we see what does and doesn't work for them, we learn what could help us improve our own service quality and communications skills. Let's take a look at how to apply these lessons in our own lives.

The Basics

The first part of the book revolves around the fundamentals of a good customer transaction: making a good first impression, listening to your customers, not hassling or being rude to people, and avoiding negative expectations.

These guiding principles seem pretty obvious at first glance, don't they? They sound like variations on a basic theme of being a nice, helpful person. But the stories in this book attempt to put these guidelines in a much more practical and realistic light, revolving around one key fact: They all go against our human nature. Think carefully about how we tend to react to most situations in our lives, and you will see why customer service often isn't what it should be:

- Instead of saying things designed to make a good first impression on people, we tend to "be ourselves."

- When we are faced with an endless stream of transactions from people, or have heard the same questions dozens of times a day, we tend not to listen to customers, focusing instead on "moving things along."

- When people do things that inconvenience us, we tend to react with annoyance.

- When enough things go wrong, we tend to set more boundaries and limits on people in the future.

Because of this human nature, we usually can't just set out to be "nice" and expect great service to happen—because this desire to be nice only lasts until our next challenging customer, difficult situation, or bad hair day. This natural split between how we think we should ideally behave, versus our natural, instinctive reactions when we are face-to-face with actual people, dates back to our prehistoric survival instincts. We are not biologically designed to give other people excellent customer service. We are designed to protect ourselves and our interests.

This means that excellent service really begins with knowing how we naturally react, and then planning and rehearsing different reactions—such as a good opening greeting, the mechanics of listening attentively to the same questions you've heard all day, and positive ways to tell people to keep their little darlings away from your fragile merchandise. In a sense, it is a little like acting. And with practice, the basics of a good customer transaction can become a natural part of who we are in front of other people.

On the Front Lines

With the basics in hand, we then move to the "advanced course" for being on the front lines with customers: avoiding confrontation with a prickly person, learning the mechanics of a good service transaction, shining when things go wrong, learning that silence isn't golden, and focusing your attention on the customer. Each of these techniques on its own will help you improve specific aspects of a customer transaction, and when taken in sum total, they can dramatically change the way that customers perceive and react to you:

- When a customer is rude, demanding, or arrogant, human nature may lead us to respond in kind—but when you learn how to speak to the wants and needs of such people, their defenses often break down and they become cooperative and helpful.

- Understanding the mechanics common to any customer transaction—like calling people by name, getting to know their preferences, noticing and acknowledging their families, and thanking them—will in turn build customer relationships that lead to good feelings and increased business.

- In difficult situations, when you speak to a customer's interest instead of getting defensive—even if it is as simple as acknowledging how the other person feels—you go a long way toward defusing the situation.

- When responding to a customer, use words and phrases that fit your own personality, but avoid silence, which conveys a sense of rudeness, inattention, and disrespect.

- Overcoming our natural tendency to focus on ourselves, and keeping our attention on the customer, is an essential component of a good service experience.

The common denominator in each case is that they are techniques, not just feelings. Good service, like good baseball or good violin playing, is a skill that takes learning and practice. At the same time, learning the fundamentals of good service has one key advantage over most other endeavors: When you become good at serving the public, you gain a set of interpersonal and leadership skills that affect nearly every other area of your life!

R-E-S-P-E-C-T

The next part of the book moves beyond the core skills of service into perhaps the most important aspect of an encounter between yourself and other people—respecting them as fellow human beings with needs and feelings. The stories in this section touch on how you treat people, not letting product superiority or expertise turn into arrogance, respecting diversity, and using positive reinforcement. Taken together, they provide a game plan for changing your perceptions and relationships with others:

- It can be all too easy to see customers as a faceless mass of people with annoying needs and problems, but when you take steps to show them respect they'll often become your fans and partners.

- When having a good product or service leads you to become self-centered and ignore customers' feelings, it could cost you business activity and customers.

- Diversity is a fact of life in human society. This means that personal biases toward race, gender, ethnicity, age, or style of dress have no place in customer service, or for that matter in life itself.

- When you do or say things that make your customers feel good—such as complimenting them or doing them an unexpected favor—you create a sense of positive reinforcement that keeps these customers coming back.

The stories in this section have two objectives for your work with customers. The first and most obvious one is that customers are people who deserve respect and attention for what they need—and more important, who they are. This sense of respect bridges the gap between simple customer service and long-term customer relationships, which in turn plays a key role in the success of your workplace.

The second objective is more subtle, and perhaps more important: When you learn to view people and their needs with respect, and treat them accordingly, you enrich your own life in ways that you may never have imagined. Your ability to make positive connections with people can go far beyond customer service. When you have the knack for creating great relationships with others, you create a win-win situation that benefits both the customer, in the present moment, and your career and personal life in the long term.

Service Strategy

The personal skills that make for good customer service exist within the larger context of getting and keeping customers for your organization. The stories in this section look at some of these strategy issues, such as learning what your customers want and need, setting and meeting appropriate expectations, understanding and respecting your own unique personality, and giving people more than they expect. Each strategy forms a fundamental part of creating the customer relationships that are the lifeblood of your organization:

- No amount of customer service skills can overcome the failure to give people what they want and need. (I call this the "fried possum" principle, because if you open a restaurant that serves nothing but fried possum, it probably isn't the fault of your service quality that no one is showing up!) When you get into your customers' heads and learn what makes them want to do business with you, you can align your product and your service quality with the demands of your marketplace.

- Setting customer expectations is a key part of what makes them happy, and what makes them come back. When you learn to undercommit and overdeliver, you do a better job of meeting customer expectations, so you'll build much greater levels of customer satisfaction into your business.

- The personalities of your customers will vary. After all, they're people! Likewise, you don't have to be a perky, happy person to give people great service. And when you hire people to serve others, realize that a diverse mix of personalities will better reflect the needs and sensibilities of the people they serve.

- Meeting expectations is important, but going the extra mile when appropriate can dramatically set you apart from your competition. When you consistently give people 110 percent, you share the secret of many organizations that consistently dominate their markets.

It is impossible to have good customer service without customers, so strategic steps to attract and retain customers are essential to any organization's service strategy. Combined with your good service skills, they form the backbone of a customer-driven environment that succeeds for people on both sides of the counter.

You and Your Service Team

The book's final section looks at what is perhaps the most critical issue of all in customer service—the relationship between managers and their employees:

- When you have a workplace that is too focused on rules, procedures, and compliance with policy, bad service is usually the inevitable result. While there are boundaries for everything, there is a difference between reasonable guidelines and an inflexible rat's nest of rules and procedures.

- Working with customers is hard enough. Being constantly criticized by your boss makes it even harder, because it will encourage you to want to keep out of trouble, not please your customers. Positive, strength-based coaching—which, sadly, is more often talked about than practiced—is essential for making positive changes in your team's performance.

Your employees are, in a very real sense, your customers. How you treat them will be reflected in how they treat "the other" customers. There is a simple litmus test to tell how effectively you are coaching people who serve the public: What do you say to employees who get frustrated with a customer and end up saying something they shouldn't? If you respond with criticism, you are probably accomplishing little more than breeding frustration and resentment. But if instead you say something like, "I can tell that customer frustrated you. Let's do some role playing and I'll show you how I handle these situations," then congratulations—you get it!

In Closing

Our closing point—and the key point of this book—is that good service should be fun! These funny stories are designed to show you and your team how easy it is, with a little knowledge and practice, to dramatically change your service quality and the reactions you get from customers, and above all, how much fun it is to come to work every morning.

The lessons in these stories aren't just platitudes. They are based on real psychological principles of how we interact with one other. They have a strong track record of improving service performance, morale, and turnover, while at the same time creating loyal and happy customers for your business or organization. Share these stories with everyone on your team, put their principles to work, and soon you will find yourself laughing all the way to the bank, literally and figuratively. Good luck and best of success!

Index

About the Author

Richard S. Gallagher is a communication skills expert and former customer service executive who heads the Point of Contact Group (www.pointofcontactgroup.com), a training and development firm in Ithaca, New York. He is the author of several books, including *Great Customer Connections: Simple Psychological Techniques That Guarantee Exceptional Service* (AMACOM, 2006) and *The Soul of an Organization* (Kaplan, 2002).